MW00884742

SENTENCE WRITING
WORKBOOK
GRADE 1

THIS BOOK
BELONGS TO

Sentence Writing Workbook Grade 1
by Whiz Kid Books

Published by Alterra Business Consulting Ltd

Copyright © 2023 Whiz Kid Books

Tips for Sentence Writing Practice

Thank you for purchasing this workbook from Whiz Kid Books. The workbook is in three sections:

1. **Complete the Sentence - Copy the word**
   a. Read the words at the top of the page with your child.
   b. Read each sentence and help them to find the word which completes the sentence and makes sense.
   c. The child copies the word in the gap using the dotted lines.
2. **Complete the Sentence - Choose the words**
   a. Read the words in each column.
   b. The child then makes a sentence by selecting one word from each column and writing the sentence on the dotted lines.
   c. Each word bank allows for 3 or more sentences
   d. Sometimes the combinations of words make a funny or silly sentence!
3. **Word Bank**

The final section is a set of 36 lessons each containing 8 words for your child to practice reading, spelling, tracing and writing. These lessons reinforce learning and help with fine motor skills, confident reading and spelling supporting their journey through Grade 1 and Grade 2.

Our complementary **Spelling Workbooks** can be found by searching for **Whiz Kid Spelling** on the Amazon store.

COMPLETE THE SENTENCE

Copy the word which finishes the sentence correctly

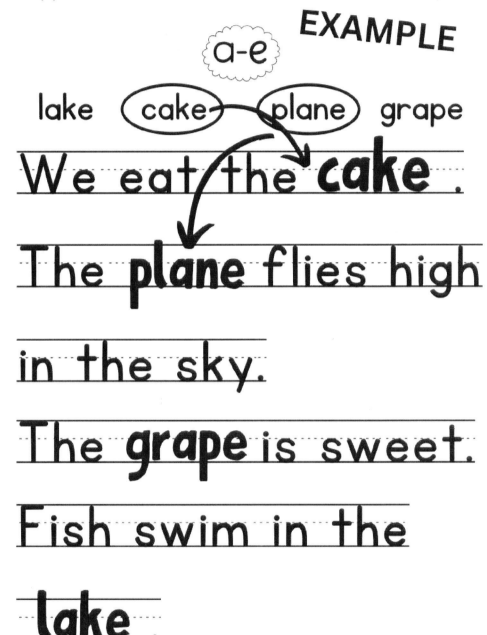

EXAMPLE

a-e

lake (cake) (plane) grape

We eat the **cake**.

The **plane** flies high

in the sky.

The **grape** is sweet.

Fish swim in the

lake.

COMPLETE THE SENTENCE

Copy the word which finishes the sentence correctly

a-e

lake   cake   plane   grape

We eat the _____ .

The _____ flies high

in the sky.

The _____ is sweet.

Fish swim in the

_____

_____ .

COMPLETE THE SENTENCE

Copy the word which finishes the sentence correctly

-ai-

stain   train   paint   rail   mail

The _____ made a

_____

_____ .

The _____ was late.

The _____ is on

the _____ .

COMPLETE THE SENTENCE

Copy the word which finishes the sentence correctly

a-e

play   pay   day gray bay

We go to the bay.

The _____ flies high

in the sky.

I _____ all _____ long.

We _____ in the shop.

Dad's shirt is _____ .

COMPLETE THE SENTENCE

Copy the word which finishes the sentence correctly

-ea-

leaf   tea   sea   peas   read

The _____ is green.

We swim in the _____

I can _____ a book.

The _____ is hot.

We _____ in the shop

_____ are green.

COMPLETE THE SENTENCE

Copy the word which finishes the sentence correctly

(i-e)

time   bite   ride   pie   lime

It's _____ for _____ .

I _____ the _____ .

We _____ the bus.

The _____ is hot.

What _____ is it?

COMPLETE THE SENTENCE

Copy the word which finishes the sentence correctly

o-e

pole   note   stove   robe   nose

The _____ is tall.

The _____ is hot.

My _____ is red.

I can read the _____.

I have a blue _____.

COMPLETE THE SENTENCE

Copy the word which finishes the sentence correctly

-sh-

shop   fish   shirt   sheep   shed

The _____ is open.

My _____ is white.

The _____ is in the sea.

We see the _____ .

We play in the _____ .

COMPLETE THE SENTENCE

Choose one word from each column to make sentences.
Write the words on the guide lines below.

EXAMPLE

A	little	green	ball
The	big	red	cap
	small		

A big red ball.

The small green

cap.

The big red cap.

COMPLETE THE SENTENCE

Choose one word from each column to make sentences.
Write the words on the guide lines below.

EXAMPLE

A	little	green	ball
The	big	red	cap
	small		

A small red ball.

The little green cap.

A big green ball.

The small red cap.

COMPLETE THE SENTENCE

Choose one word from each column to make sentences.
Write the words on the guide lines below.

A	little	green	ball
The	big	red	cap
	small		

COMPLETE THE SENTENCE

Choose one word from each column to make sentences.
Write the words on the guide lines below.

The	car	is	red
	door		yellow
	boat		blue

COMPLETE THE SENTENCE

Choose one word from each column to make sentences.
Write the words on the guide lines below.

The	man	ran	fast
A	dog	walks	slowly
		eats	

COMPLETE THE SENTENCE

Choose one word from each column to make sentences.
Write the words on the guide lines below.

I	write	the	word
You	read	a	letter
They	copy		

COMPLETE THE SENTENCE

Choose one word from each column to make sentences.
Write the words on the guide lines below.

The	cat	is	white
My	dog		black
Your			brown

COMPLETE THE SENTENCE

Choose one word from each column to make sentences. Write the words on the guide lines below.

The	grass	is	green
His	flower	was	dry
Her	pan		

COMPLETE THE SENTENCE

Choose one word from each column to make sentences.
Write the words on the guide lines below.

The	fat	pig	hops
My	thin	goat	jumps
	old		

COMPLETE THE SENTENCE

Choose one word from each column to make sentences.
Write the words on the guide lines below.

We	play	a	game
They	win	the	race
You	like		

COMPLETE THE SENTENCE

Choose one word from each column to make sentences.
Write the words on the guide lines below.

My	nose	is	hot
His	head	was	cold
Her			

COMPLETE THE SENTENCE

Choose one word from each column to make sentences.
Write the words on the guide lines below.

They	took	the	spoon
You	wash	my	car
		his	

COMPLETE THE SENTENCE

Choose one word from each column to make sentences.
Write the words on the guide lines below.

The	hole	was	deep
A	pool	is	dark
	snow		

COMPLETE THE SENTENCE

Choose one word from each column to make sentences.
Write the words on the guide lines below.

Shall	we	go	out?
Can	I	climb	up?
May			in?

COMPLETE THE SENTENCE

Choose one word from each column to make sentences.
Write the words on the guide lines below.

The	brown	cow	eats
A	big	sheep	

COMPLETE THE SENTENCE

Choose one word from each column to make sentences.
Write the words on the guide lines below.

He	has	long	hair
She		nice	socks

COMPLETE THE SENTENCE

Choose one word from each column to make sentences.
Write the words on the guide lines below.

The	moon	is	full
	sun	was	round
			hot

COMPLETE THE SENTENCE

Choose one word from each column to make sentences.
Write the words on the guide lines below.

I	look	down	deep
You	see	up	high
We			

COMPLETE THE SENTENCE

Choose one word from each column to make sentences.
Write the words on the guide lines below.

I	wash	with	water
We	drink	the	soap
			tea

COMPLETE THE SENTENCE

Choose one word from each column to make sentences.
Write the words on the guide lines below.

My	bug	is	shy
His	fox		free
	pet		

COMPLETE THE SENTENCE

Choose one word from each column to make sentences.
Write the words on the guide lines below.

The	man	works	hard
	woman		slowly
	girl		

COMPLETE THE SENTENCE

Choose one word from each column to make sentences.
Write the words on the guide lines below.

Do	you	like	cake?
Can		eat	apples?
Will			

COMPLETE THE SENTENCE

Choose one word from each column to make sentences.
Write the words on the guide lines below.

The	duck	floats	well
	ship	stops	quickly
	boat	is	yellow

COMPLETE THE SENTENCE

Choose one word from each column to make sentences.
Write the words on the guide lines below.

The	clock	was	wrong
My	answer		right
Your			

COMPLETE THE SENTENCE

Choose one word from each column to make sentences.
Write the words on the guide lines below.

The	wise	old	owl
A	friendly	young	horse
	naughty		

COMPLETE THE SENTENCE

Choose one word from each column to make sentences.
Write the words on the guide lines below.

Where	is	the	pen?
What		a	wood?
How			town?

COMPLETE THE SENTENCE

Choose one word from each column to make sentences.
Write the words on the guide lines below.

The	ant	bit	me
	bee	stung	him
			her

COMPLETE THE SENTENCE

Choose one word from each column to make sentences.
Write the words on the guide lines below.

Swim	in	the	pool
Play		a	park
Jump			sea

COMPLETE THE SENTENCE

Choose one word from each column to make sentences.
Write the words on the guide lines below.

The	big	bus	stopped	quickly
	small	car	crashed	loudly
	green		went	

COMPLETE THE SENTENCE

Choose one word from each column to make sentences.
Write the words on the guide lines below.

The	smart	girl	sang	loudly
	clever	boy	whispered	quietly
		children	shouted	

COMPLETE THE SENTENCE

Choose one word from each column to make sentences. Write the words on the guide lines below.

We	fed	the	animals	today
I	stroked		pets	yesterday
Jack			chicken	

COMPLETE THE SENTENCE

Choose one word from each column to make sentences.
Write the words on the guide lines below.

The	small	baby	cries	loudly
	little	child	shouts	
	tiny			

COMPLETE THE SENTENCE

Choose one word from each column to make sentences.
Write the words on the guide lines below.

I	suck	the	green	sweet
You	try		yellow	ice
			pink	

COMPLETE THE SENTENCE

Choose one word from each column to make sentences.
Write the words on the guide lines below.

Show	me	the	huge	boat
Give		a	long	stick
Hand				

COMPLETE THE SENTENCE

Choose one word from each column to make sentences.
Write the words on the guide lines below.

The	girl	kicks	the	ball
	boy	drops		top
		spins		

COMPLETE THE SENTENCE

Choose one word from each column to make sentences.
Write the words on the guide lines below.

The	clown	is	very	happy
	father		not	sad
	mother			funny

COMPLETE THE SENTENCE

Choose one word from each column to make sentences.
Write the words on the guide lines below.

We	go	out	on	Monday
They		in		Friday
I		up		Sunday

COMPLETE THE SENTENCE

Choose one word from each column to make sentences.
Write the words on the guide lines below.

On	Tuesday	Tom	plays
	Thursday	Sarah	dances
	Saturday	Jo	shops

COMPLETE THE SENTENCE

Choose one word from each column to make sentences.
Write the words on the guide lines below.

My	sister	is	very	kind
	brother		quite	fast
	cousin		really	strong

COMPLETE THE SENTENCE

Choose one word from each column to make sentences.
Write the words on the guide lines below.

We	sit	on	the	rug
	stay	in		hut
	lie			

WORD BANK
GRADE 1

Lesson 1

Read & Learn	Trace	Write
the	the	
of	of	
and	and	
that	that	
cat	cat	
mat	mat	
sat	sat	
hat	hat	

Lesson 2

Read & Learn	Trace	Write
to	to	
in	in	
is	is	
you	you	
man	man	
can	can	
ran	ran	
pan	pan	

Lesson 3

Read & Learn	Trace	Write
than	than	
it	it	
he	he	
was	was	
map	map	
cap	cap	
nap	nap	
tap	tap	

Lesson 4

Read & Learn	Trace	Write
for	for	
on	on	
are	are	
as	as	
back	back	
sack	sack	
black	black	
snack	snack	

Lesson 5

Read & Learn	Trace	Write
with	with	
his	his	
they	they	
pit	pit	
sit	sit	
hit	hit	
bit	bit	
fit	fit	

Lesson 6

Read & Learn	Trace	Write
at	at	
be	be	
this	this	
have	have	
big	big	
pig	pig	
dig	dig	
wig	wig	

Lesson 7

Read & Learn	Trace	Write
from	from	
or	or	
one	one	
had	had	
thin	thin	
pin	pin	
skin	skin	
spin	spin	

Lesson 8

Read & Learn	Trace	Write
by	by	
words	words	
but	but	
not	not	
sick	sick	
kick	kick	
brick	brick	
stick	stick	

Lesson 9

Read & Learn	Trace	Write
what	what	
all	all	
were	were	
we	we	
hot	hot	
pot	pot	
lot	lot	
not	not	

Lesson 10

Read & Learn	Trace	Write
when	when	
your	your	
pop	pop	
said	said	
mop	mop	
top	top	
hop	hop	
drop	drop	

Lesson 11

Read & Learn	Trace	Write
there	there	
use	use	
an	an	
each	each	
job	job	
mob	mob	
rob	rob	
cob	cob	

Lesson 12

Read & Learn	Trace	Write
which	which	
she	she	
do	do	
how	how	
sock	sock	
rock	rock	
block	block	
clock	clock	

Lesson 13

Read & Learn	Trace	Write
their	their	
if	if	
will	will	
up	up	
cut	cut	
nut	nut	
hut	hut	
shut	shut	

Lesson 14

Read & Learn	Trace	Write
other	other	
about	about	
out	out	
many	many	
bug	bug	
hug	hug	
mug	mug	
rug	rug	

Lesson 15

Read & Learn	Trace	Write
then	then	
them	them	
these	these	
so	so	
sun	sun	
run	run	
fun	fun	
bun	bun	

Lesson 16

Read & Learn	Trace	Write
some	some	
her	her	
would	would	
make	make	
duck	duck	
luck	luck	
suck	suck	
stuck	stuck	

Lesson 17

Read & Learn	Trace	Write
like	like	
him	him	
into	into	
time	time	
pet	pet	
get	get	
wet	wet	
let	let	

Lesson 18

Copy	Trace	Write
has	has	
look	look	
two	two	
more	more	
red	red	
bed	bed	
fed	fed	
sled	sled	

Lesson 19

Read & Learn	Trace	Write
write	write	
go	go	
see	see	
number	number	
men	men	
hen	hen	
pen	pen	
ten	ten	

Lesson 20

Read & Learn	Trace	Write
no	no	
bell	bell	
could	could	
people	people	
tell	tell	
fell	fell	
sell	sell	
well	well	

Lesson 21

Read & Learn	Trace	Write
my	my	
ant	ant	
first	first	
water	water	
bad	bad	
bat	bat	
glad	glad	
mad	mad	

Lesson 22

Read & Learn	Trace	Write
been	been	
called	called	
who	who	
oil	oil	
win	win	
lip	lip	
kid	kid	
ship	ship	

Lesson 23

Read & Learn	Trace	Write
dog	dog	
now	now	
find	find	
long	long	
mom	mom	
fox	fox	
chop	chop	
shop	shop	

Lesson 24

Read & Learn	Trace	Write
down	down	
day	day	
did	did	
set	set	
bus	bus	
truck	truck	
must	must	
cup	cup	

Lesson 25

Read & Learn	Trace	Write
come	come	
made	made	
may	may	
part	part	
web	web	
legs	legs	
less	less	
shell	shell	

Lesson 26

Read & Learn	Trace	Write
game	come	
page	made	
race	may	
tape	part	
name	web	
shake	legs	
tame	less	
animal	shell	

Lesson 27

Read & Learn	Trace	Write
way	way	
pay	pay	
stay	stay	
clay	clay	
play	play	
tray	tray	
roots	roots	
tree	tree	

Lesson 28

Read & Learn	Trace	Write
nice	nice	
drive	drive	
mine	mine	
wise	wise	
dine	dine	
five	five	
lime	lime	
next	next	

Lesson 31

Read & Learn	Trace	Write
low	low	
show	show	
grow	grow	
flow	flow	
show	show	
blow	blow	
above	above	
below	below	

Lesson 32

Read & Learn	Trace	Write
coat	coat	
boat	boat	
float	float	
soak	soak	
load	load	
soap	soap	
stop	stop	
trip	trip	

Lesson 33

Read & Learn	Trace	Write
hook	hook	
took	took	
good	good	
stood	stood	
wood	wood	
foot	foot	
gas	gas	
heat	heat	

Lesson 34

Read & Learn	Trace	Write
cow	cow	
low	low	
brown	brown	
town	town	
clown	clown	
tower	tower	
sure	sure	
vote	vote	

Lesson 35

Read & Learn	Trace	Write
moon	moon	
spoon	spoon	
tooth	tooth	
broom	broom	
roof	roof	
pool	pool	
huge	huge	
ice	ice	

Lesson 36

Read & Learn	Trace	Write
deep	deep	
feel	feel	
green	green	
seed	seed	
need	need	
free	free	
grass	grass	
summer	summer	

Thank you for purchasing this workbook from Whiz Kid Books. There are many more useful workbooks for helping your children succeed at school.

Find them by using the QR code below. Simply hold your mobile phone camera over the code and click on the link which will take you to our Amazon store.

Other topics from Whiz Kid Books
- Telling the Time
- Sight Words
- Math Timed Tests
  - Addition
  - Subtraction
  - Multiplication
  - Division
- Fractions & Decimals
- Geometry
- Math Word Problems

As a new small educational publisher, we would really welcome your review on Amazon. Thank you!

Made in United States
North Haven, CT
20 February 2024

48977919R00048